WERE YOU THERE WHEN THEY CRUCIFIED MY LORD?

Six Plays for the Lenten Season Featuring Persons at the Passion

W. Carl Bogard, Th.M., D.D.

ABINGDON PRESS
Nashville

WERE YOU THERE WHEN THEY CRUCIFIED MY LORD?

Copyright © 1997 by Abingdon Press

Scripture quotations noted NIV are from the Holy Bible, New International Version. Copyright © 1973, 1978, 1984 by International Bible Society. Used by permission of Zondervan Bible Publishers.

Those designated NRSV are from the New Revised Standard Version of the Bible, copyright © 1989 by the Division of Christian Education, National Council of the Churches of Christ in the United States of America. Used by permission.

ISBN 0-687-03192-3

97 98 99 00 01 02 03 04 —10 9 8 7 6 5 4 3 2 1

MANUFACTURED IN THE UNITED STATES OF AMERICA

Contents

Foreword

The history of these plays goes back to the early 1940s when Carl Bogard wrote them for use in worship at the First Presbyterian Church (now the Covenant Presbyterian Church) in Butler, Pennsylvania, where he was pastor. As a teenager in that church, I, along with twenty other members of our youth group, participated in a production of the plays.

In the early 1950s, as a student at McCormick Theological Seminary in Chicago, I wanted to use the plays with the youth of the First Presbyterian Church in Wilmette, Illinois, where I was doing field education. I asked Carl for a set of scripts, which he quickly and gladly supplied. My collaborator in Wilmette was G. Daniel Little, also a student at McCormick, and now my husband.

For the past forty-five years, my pastor husband and I have used these plays in every church where we have served: in small congregations in the Dockland area of London, England; in an urban, interracial congregation in a public housing community in Pittsburgh, Pennsylvania; in West Side Presbyterian Church in Ridgewood, New Jersey; in First Presbyterian Church in Ithaca, New York; at McCormick Seminary (forty years later!); and, most recently, at the Village Church in Prairie Village, Kansas—in a contemporary service of Communion, at a Lenten breakfast, and with a youth group.

I have seen over these years that different people in many different settings—both actors and audiences—have been moved (sometimes to tears) by these unique, biblically based plays. I personally have been affected by them profoundly, not only as a teenager but each time I work with them.

We live in a media age. Drama provides an opportunity to reenact these sacred stories from God's Word within our communities of faith. These plays have never failed in fifty years of use, for they bring the persons of the Passion alive in familiar yet contemporary terms.

It is very satisfying to me that, at long last, with their publication they are now available to educators, pastors, professors, youth leaders, women's association leaders, small groups, and congregations everywhere. May God bless you in your use of them. May you come closer to Christ as you reenact the experience of those who knew him first.

— Joan McCafferty Little

Acknowledgments

For these dramas I am indebted primarily to him
  who "bore *in his body* my sins upon the tree."
I am also indebted to his disciples,
    so inspired by his sacrifice that they recorded
    what happened to him and to them.
I thank him for the meaning of his cross
    to all his people down through the centuries.
I express gratitude
    to my parents for bringing me up on the Bible,
      and my seminary professors, especially
        Dr. Andrew W. Blackwood, my graduate scholar-
          ship advisor, for helping me to interpret it
            for everyday living.
I appreciate all the actors,
    many of them first-timers,
      for daring to portray their devotion on the "stage."
I am thankful for Joan McCafferty Little and her husband
    G. Daniel Little for their enthusiastic support of these plays
      wherever they served and their initiative in getting
        the plays published.
I am grateful to the publisher for believing the plays
    may help others respond to the cross.
For a half century of devotion I am indebted to my wife,
    Alice Hollowell Bogard, for expressing her love by
      typing, retyping, and re-retyping the scripts
        and for making of them a work of art.

—W. Carl Bogard, Th.M., D.D.

The Leader—Peter

Characters
    PETER, The Leader of the Twelve Apostles
    JOHN, the Beloved Disciple
    JESUS
    MALCHUS
    PORTRESS
    SERVANT of the High Priest

Resources
Prop: Big-blade knife
Music Suggestions: "In the Hour of Trial", "Were You There" (background interlude), "Just As I Am"
Sound Effect: Tape of rooster crowing (available at most radio stations)
Literature Suggestion: "The Look," "The Meaning of the Look," E. B. Browning

<u>SCENE 1</u>

Setting: The Upper Room in Mark's home where a long table flanked by two benches is set horizontally.
Time: Near sunset Thursday evening of Passion Week
Scripture: Mark 14:17-20, 22-25

JOHN:	*(Entering downstage center as Peter is arranging the table with his back to the audience)* Everything ready, Peter?
PETER:	*(Turning)* Sure, John. I don't think I forgot anything.
JOHN:	Good. *(Checking the table, touching lamb and licking his finger)* The lamb, the wine, the wafers.
PETER:	I wonder why the rabbi often chooses you and me to do special things for him. Have you noticed that?
JOHN:	Yes, I have. I've wondered, too, but haven't come up with any good answers. It's a little easier to guess in your case. There's always something happening when you're around.
PETER:	*(Sitting on end of bench in front of table)* I've got a gut feeling that there's going to be something special about this Passover. This afternoon he didn't tell us we were going to have it here at Mark's house. He told us to follow a man carrying a pitcher of water. Every man in Jerusalem draws water for the unleavened bread. It could have been anybody other than Mark carrying water when we came by.

JOHN:	*(Having sat on the other end of the bench in front of the table)* Well, it worked out all right. Of course, after all the things we've seen him do, I don't suppose we should be surprised any more, but I still am.
PETER:	Same here. *(Edging closer)* But do you know what I think?
JOHN:	I couldn't guess. In fact, sometimes I'm not sure you think.
PETER:	I do think—and I'll just bet he's getting ready for the coming of his Kingdom, whatever that means.
JOHN:	Maybe so. But, as always, we'll leave that to him, and he'll tell us when he's ready.
PETER:	I know. But if his Kingdom is coming, I want to do my part. He's sort of made us his lieutenants, and I want to be good and ready to act like one.
JOHN:	More like a sergeant, I'd say. I'm not worried about you doing your part, Peter. You always do, right up to your elbows.
PETER:	Well, I try. I think I'm ready for action. *(Showing his knife, a dagger with a large blade)*
JOHN:	What's that for, Peter?
PETER:	Never can tell. I may need it. *(Pocketing knife)* I just know that something's going to happen.
JOHN:	Well, I can't help feeling you've got some mixed-up ideas, but who am I to try to change you now? *(Pauses, listens, then continues)* They're coming. I hear his voice! *(Rising)*
PETER:	Right. *(Going downstage to meet them)* Hello! Come in and bring your appetites.
JESUS:	Is everything ready, Peter? *(Entering downstage from aisle)*
PETER:	We believe so, Rabbi.
JESUS:	Did you find this guest room well furnished, and the food and drink on hand?
PETER:	*(Moving behind table)* Yes, Mark had everything all set, and I think we've got a good cut of lamb.
JESUS:	Good. *(Warmly)* It's such a comfort to be among my best friends at a time like this. *(Sitting on center of front bench)*
PETER:	*(Sitting center on bench behind table)* That goes double for us too, Rabbi.

JESUS:	Yes, I believe it does. Rest, my friends. *(John sits to left on front bench)* For many reasons I have looked forward to having this meal with you before I suffer. It is the last Passover—my very last supper.
PETER:	Does all this mean that your Kingdom is coming now, Rabbi?
JESUS:	Yes, it does. As a sign of it, take this bread as my body which will be given for you. *(John receives the bread, then Peter)* This cup is the new covenant in my blood which will be poured out for you. *(John takes cup first, then hands it to Peter)* Whenever you eat this bread and drink this cup, you will remember my death and its purpose until I return forever. What hurts now is that one of you will betray me.
PETER:	What?
JESUS:	Yes.
PETER:	Not me, is it, Rabbi?
JESUS:	No, Peter.
JOHN:	I?
JESUS:	No, John.
PETER:	*(Whispers across the table to John)* Ask him who it is.
JOHN:	*(Whispers)* Who is it?
JESUS:	*(To John)* The one to whom I will give the piece of bread I dipped in the meat juice.
PETER:	*(To John)* Who did he say it would be?
JOHN:	The man who gets the dipped bread.
PETER:	So far we've all had some, haven't we?
JOHN:	Not this last one.
PETER:	*(Rising to his feet)* Judas! Now where is Judas going?
JOHN:	You *are* more than a little thick now and then. Let's just say it's to buy some food, Peter. The markets are closed tomorrow.
PETER:	*(Sitting and leaning forward)* Oh, sure, I forgot. *(Pause)* Rabbi, if your Kingdom is coming soon, who are going to be its leaders?
JESUS:	Those who serve most, Peter.
PETER:	Those who serve most?

JESUS:	Yes, you eleven have been faithful to me. You will have a share in my Kingdom. You will sit on thrones ruling the Twelve Tribes of Israel.
PETER:	*(Beaming)* Ah-ha! Well, now—ruling the Twelve Tribes! Not bad!
JESUS:	I have prayed—especially for you, *Simon*, that your faith won't fail.
PETER:	Why do you call me by my old name, *Simon*? I thought you named me Peter, "the Rock," and convinced the fellows you weren't talking about my head. You know you can count on me, rabbi. Others may desert you. I never will.
JESUS:	All right then, *Peter*. But let me tell you, Peter, that before the rooster crows twice in the morning you will deny me three times.
PETER:	*(Standing)* Not a chance. Even if I have to die for you *(fingering knife in pocket)*, I won't fail you. What do the rest of you say?
JOHN:	You speak for all of us, Peter.
PETER:	Hear that, Rabbi?
JESUS:	Your zest is strong, Peter, but don't be too sure of yourself.
PETER:	*(Showing his knife)* Well, I'm ready for action.
JESUS:	*(Smiling sympathetically)* Yes, Peter. Let us go.
PETER:	Where, Rabbi?
JESUS:	To the Garden of Gethsemane.
PETER:	*(Leading downstage)* Let's go.

(They exit downstage, up the aisle)

SCENE 2

Setting: The Garden of Gethsemane
Time: The same night near the eleventh hour. *(Jesus and his disciples are approaching up the center aisle)*
Scripture: Mark 14:32-46; John 18:10-11

JESUS:	Here we are again, my friends, for the last time. Please watch here while I go and pray. *(Peter and John stop halfway up aisle)* Peter, will you come with me?
PETER:	Yes, Rabbi.

JESUS:	John with James, too. I need your company *very* much. *(Entering downstage center, with the two following. James is imagined or may be portrayed in person)* My soul is very sorrowful, even unto death. I am going a little farther to pray alone. Stay here and watch with me.
PETER:	Count on us! We'll do anything we can for you, Rabbi.
JESUS:	Don't be concerned about me. Look out for yourselves. Watch what happens and pray for strength to face it.
PETER:	Leave it to us. Nothing can bother us. *(Jesus moves upstage. Peter and John lean on supports at right and left of stage)* You know, the moon seems close enough to touch it.
JOHN:	It's so quiet and calm tonight—and it's hard to believe that this night may be different from all the other nights we've ever seen.
PETER:	I wonder when Judas is coming back. *(Looking downstage into distance)* Hmm, there seems to be a torch parade in the city. See that glow of light against the sky near the temple? *(Fingering blade in pocket)* You never can tell what may happen around there during the Passover.
JOHN:	*(Thinking in a deeper vein as he sits)* The rabbi seems terribly disturbed tonight.
PETER:	*(Sitting)* Yes, he seems to need our support because here *we* are again. I still wonder why he wants *us*.
JOHN:	I still don't know, Peter, but I hope we're worthy of his trust. Tonight he seems more like a brother than ever before.
JESUS:	*(Listening intently)* My Father, if it be possible, let this cup pass from me. *(Pause)* Nevertheless, not my will but thine be done.
PETER:	*(Puzzled)* What does he mean by that?
JOHN:	Patience, Peter. Time will tell.
PETER:	*(Yawning)* I wonder if we'll get *any* rest tonight? I'm tired. *(Looking at the moon)* It must be close to midnight. I'm likely to drop off any minute now. If the rabbi needs me, call me. Hmm, that glow is getting brighter. *(Peter slumbers. Jesus returns and arouses him.)*
JESUS:	Peter!
PETER:	Yes, Rabbi! Hey! John, James, wake up! I must have nodded a little. *(John stays seated)*

JESUS:	For about an hour, Peter. Couldn't you watch with me for just that long?
PETER:	*(Rising)* Sorry, Rabbi. What are those bloody marks on your face? Has someone hurt you? *(Fingering his blade)*
JESUS:	No, not me . . . Peter. Watch and pray that *you* will not be tempted. Your spirit is willing, but the flesh can be weak.
PETER:	We'll do better this time, Rabbi. Honestly!
JESUS:	I'm not concerned for myself, but for you.
PETER:	If you need me, call! *(Looking downstage)* Look at that glow! *(Jesus repeats the same prayer. Peter goes to sleep once more. Jesus returns.)*
JESUS:	Peter! Again?
PETER:	I'm sorry . . . again. Aren't we going back to Bethany to sleep?
JESUS:	I'm never going back to Bethany. See that parade of torches coming up the path?
PETER:	Yes, who are they? *(Startled and ready)* Hey! James and John, on your feet!
JOHN:	*(Jumping)* What is it?
PETER:	A mob, coming up this way.
JOHN:	Who are they? *(To Peter)* The Temple guard? Do I see swords?
PETER:	Yes. That's the guard and they've got swords all right. Bully boys.
JESUS:	Let's go out to meet them. The betrayer is with them.
PETER:	*(Dumbfounded)* The betrayer! Who?
JESUS:	You will see. Let us go back to the other disciples. They will need us. *(Moving downstage)*
PETER:	Let's go. I'll stop him! *(Drawing his blade)*
JESUS:	*(As they move off the stage into aisle)* Put up your blade, Peter. That is not the way of my Kingdom. *(Judas enters, comes up aisle toward stage, leading the band, personified in the servant of the high priest, and kisses Jesus)*
MALCHUS:	Judas said he would kiss him.
PETER:	*(Slapping his forehead, falling back and flashing his blade)* Judas! I might have known—and with a kiss. Hey, you

	guards! Cut it out! You can't do that! Take your dirty hands off him! *(Peter strikes with his blade and lops off the ear of Malchus)*
JESUS:	*(Sternly)* Peter, put up your blade. *(Touching the injured ear)* There, Malchus, your ear is whole again.
PETER:	But I said I would stand by you, Rabbi.
JESUS:	Not by fighting! *(John moves down the aisle with Jesus)*
PETER:	Are you going, John?
JOHN:	Yes, I'm going to stay with him. He needs a lot more than knives. You coming?
PETER:	Yes, I'll come . . . later. *(Wipes blood off his blade and conceals it in his pocket. Steals back toward stage, stops, then follows haltingly down the aisle and exits)*

SCENE 3

Setting: The courtyard of the high priest
Time: Shortly after midnight on the morning of Good Friday
Scripture: Mark 14:53, 54, 66-72

(The PORTRESS is watching at the gate. The SERVANT is building a fire upstage center)

PETER:	*(Approaching stage from center aisle)* Open up, will you?
PORTRESS:	What do you want? *(She is repulsively nosy)*
PETER:	I've got some business.
PORTRESS:	What is it? You a friend of anybody in here?
PETER:	Yeah!
PORTRESS:	Of the high priest?
PETER:	*(Hedging)* Ah . . . ah . . . yes, of the high priest.
PORTRESS:	Come in.
PETER:	Thanks.
PORTRESS:	*(Sizing him up)* Oh, yes. I know about you.
PETER:	About me?
PORTRESS:	Yes.
PETER:	*(In defense)* Now, wait a minute. It must be somebody else. I've never laid eyes on you before.

13

PORTRESS:	You are the man John told me about.
PETER:	What John?
PORTRESS:	The disciple of the rabbi! *(Boring in)* You know him?
PETER:	*(Hedging)* I've met him.
PORTRESS:	I know that John, too. He came in with that crazy rabbi and the mob earlier this evening.
PETER:	*(Subduing his interest)* Where is the rabbi?
PORTRESS:	He is being cross-examined.
PETER:	You say John is up there too?
PORTRESS:	Yes. Do you want to see him?
PETER:	*(Irritated)* Well . . . yes.
PORTRESS:	I know you are the man John described to me. You are with Jesus. You want to see *him*, I know. Well, if you do, you're out of place here. The priests have tied him up. From the way the members of the Sanhedrin have poured in through this gate, he's going to have a mighty rough time.
PETER:	I don't know him. I want to see John about some important private business.
PORTRESS:	Oh? This time of day for business? All right. Come in. But I still believe you're with Jesus.
PETER:	*(Muttering to himself as he walks toward fire upstage)* It's none of her business who I want to see. *(Rooster crows and Peter halts)* Why is that rooster crowing? It's not anywhere near dawn. *(Shivering)* Boy, the air is chilly. I think I'll ease up to the fire. *(He saunters nonchalantly up to the fire where he warms himself)*. Sorta chilly this evening. *(To servant tending the fire)* You got a good fire there.
SERVANT:	*(Sarcastically)* I ought to know that. I'm hauling wood for it. Who are you?
PETER:	Nobody in particular. Just came up for the feast. Big crowd this year.
SERVANT:	Yep. One of the biggest I've ever seen. Lot of people in *this* place tonight.
PETER:	How come?
SERVANT:	Oh, they brought in that rabble-rousing rabbi tonight. They're going to try him, they tell me. His chances of getting off are not good.

14

PETER:	Where is he?
SERVANT:	What's that to you? You one of his followers?
PORTRESS:	*(Coming up)* He sure is. John told me. His name is Peter. He's one of the disciples.
PETER:	I tell you I am not, and I don't want to hear any more about it. *(Muttering to himself)* This fire is sure hot. Think I'll take a stroll around the court. *(Walks stage left)*
SERVANT:	*(To Portress, omnisciently) I* know who he is.
PORTRESS:	How do you know?
SERVANT:	I was with the gang that went up to grab the rabbi. When we were about to tie him up, this man pulled a knife and tried to kill Malchus. *Malchus is my brother.* I saw it with my own eyes. He must have his knife with him now. *(Peter looks upstage)*
PORTRESS:	I'm sure, too. Look at him trying to sneak a glimpse of Jesus.
SERVANT:	I'll put more wood on the fire. The Sanhedrin may want to warm up, although I don't see how they could get hotter. *(Peter returns toward fire)*
PORTRESS:	Here he comes again. *(Exits off left)*
PETER:	*(Rubbing his hands together)* Doesn't take long to cool off away from the fire. *(Pause)* Say, that smoke smells good. *(Sniffs)* It burns like wild locust—*(pause)*. It reminds me of the fires I used to build along the shores of Lake Galilee. I'm a fisherman.
SERVANT:	How long has it been since you fished?
PETER:	Oh, not too long.
SERVANT:	What have you been doing lately?
PETER:	Getting ready to come to the Passover. Nearly everybody up our way comes. Sure is a large crowd this year.
SERVANT:	Yes, they're all excited about this blasted rabbi. *(Pressing the issue)* You seem interested in him yourself.
PETER:	When we were coming down to Jerusalem he just happened to be in the crowd.
SERVANT:	Sure, just happened, I suppose. You are one of his disciples!
PETER:	*(Violently)* No, I am not!

15

SERVANT:	Listen here, Peter. Don't try to fool me. I have proof *(with a flourish)*. I am the brother of Malchus. *(Peter turns. Servant grabs him by the shoulders and wheels him around)* I saw you cut off his right ear. I can get him out here and prove it. I bet you've got that knife with you right now. Let's see it.
PETER:	I don't have any.
SERVANT:	Oh, yes, you do—a bloody one!
PETER:	I don't have a knife and there is no blood. I . . . I don't know him.
SERVANT:	Have you never even *heard* about Jesus?
PETER:	*(Turning away)* Well, sure, everybody has. *(Wheeling and shouting vehemently) But I don't know him!* Now let up on me. *(Peter moves downstage and, hearing the rooster crow, catches his breath)* Oh no! The second time! *(Offstage, the voice of Jesus:* "Deny me three times." *Peter stumbles off the stage, then turns and sees Jesus being led away upstage).* Rabbi! *(He beats his breast, his head falls, and he covers his eyes with his hands. His shoulders jerk, indicating he is weeping)*
JESUS:	*(Coming back on left stage with hands crossed in front of him, speaks most sympathetically)* Simon.
PETER:	*(Tossing his knife onto the stage)* Oh! My Master. *(Kneeling and bowing submission)*
JESUS:	Peter. *(Jesus exits up downstage, up aisle, with hands crossed, and Servant off right. After a moment, Peter rises and exits left.)*

The Churchman—Caiaphas

Characters

    CAIAPHAS, the high priest in Jerusalem—The Churchman, wearing a
      black pulpit robe
    ANNAS, his father-in-law
    MALCHUS, the high priest's servant, with a patch over his right ear
    JESUS
    FIVE WITNESSES (members of the Sanhedrin)
    JOSEPH
    NICODEMUS

Resources

Prop: Gavel
Music Suggestions: "Beneath the Cross of Jesus," "Strong Son of God,
    Immortal Love," "The Wake from Saul," Handel

Literature Suggestions: "The Song of a Heathen," Richard Watson Gilder;
    "The Man Christ," Theresa Lindsey

SCENE 1

Setting: The home of the high priest in Jerusalem—a meeting room where a
    large chair with a podium to one side are positioned
Time: Near midnight shortly after the betrayal in the garden
Scripture: Mark 6:1-6; 14:55-64

(Annas is seated, nervously biding his time)

CAIAPHAS:	*(Entering right with a purposeful stride)* Pilate agrees, Annas. If the rabbi proves false, Pilate will inflict the penalty. *(Throughout, he is tense, conscientious, and official, a good man trying hard to do a good job in a Catch-22 situation)*
ANNAS:	*(Confidently)* The governor has to work with us.
CAIAPHAS:	Judas should be here soon with the rabbi. Let's think ahead about the trial.
ANNAS:	Yes, everything must be in order. We want to keep the Sanhedrin unified and running smoothly.
CAIAPHAS:	A few members like Joseph and Nicodemus may object.
ANNAS:	Yes. They will check every legal step. They believe in the rabbi.
CAIAPHAS:	*(Honestly and fervently)* I do not see how they can. Son of man, yes. But Son of God, no.

17

ANNAS:	How could a carpenter be the Messiah?
CAIAPHAS:	I cannot see how. So I must protect the people from him. As president of the Sanhedrin this year, I feel responsible for them.
ANNAS:	He even speaks against the Temple.
CAIAPHAS:	So I have heard.
ANNAS:	And without the Temple what would happen to our religion?
CAIAPHAS:	Even if it costs his life, we must save the House of God.
ANNAS:	Without it all is lost.
CAIAPHAS:	We cannot have the formal trial before daybreak. That's the law.
ANNAS:	Right. False messiahship carries the death sentence. That requires trial by day, not night.
CAIAPHAS:	Yet, if he proves false, he must be out of the way before sunset this evening when the Sabbath begins. This puts us under tremendous pressure of time, but we must keep the Sabbath holy.
ANNAS:	What witnesses do you have?
CAIAPHAS:	I have sent Malchus after members of the Sanhedrin.
ANNAS:	How long ago?
CAIAPHAS:	About half an hour.
ANNAS:	He should be back by now.
CAIAPHAS:	He should. *(Uncomfortably)* I'm a bit uneasy about him.
ANNAS:	How so? He's your servant.
CAIAPHAS:	He admires the rabbi for healing his ear. One of the followers slashed it during the arrest earlier tonight.
ANNAS:	The rabbi is helpful to some.
CAIAPHAS:	But this does not make him the Son of God. Everyone is helpful at times. *(Pause)* I told Malchus not to bother Joseph and Nicodemus.
ANNAS:	But you are not sure of him, you say.
CAIAPHAS:	He will do what I tell him. But they may hear of the assembly and come anyway.
ANNAS:	If they do, welcome them. They are fine men. They will support the truth.

18

CAIAPHAS:	They may testify for it. Two witnesses must agree.
ANNAS:	And their evidence must hold before Pilate.
CAIAPHAS:	True. If the Sanhedrin finds the rabbi false, we still have the Roman governor to convince.
ANNAS:	He agreed to go along with us, you said.
CAIAPHAS:	Yes, but you can never be sure of him. If he takes a notion the rabbi is not false, he may overrule the Sanhedrin. This will upset the people, the Temple, our religion. Through the centuries we have protected them from paganism and atheism. I must protect them now.
ANNAS:	*(Listening off left and rising nervously)* I hear the guards coming.
CAIAPHAS:	*(Rising)* It is not yet three o'clock. What can we do between now and dawn? Malchus does not yet have the Sanhedrin here.
ANNAS:	*(With mastery)* I shall have the rabbi led to my house. I will cross-examine him a moment. In the meantime, assemble the Sanhedrin and check their testimony. Two members must have the same evidence. *(Exit left)*

(Malchus enters downstage from aisle. Throughout, he is a defender of Jesus)

CAIAPHAS:	*(Anxiously)* How many members do you have?
MALCHUS:	*(Slurring his words)* I don't know. I woke them up. Some are coming now.
CAIAPHAS:	*(With concern)* Did Joseph and Nicodemus come?
MALCHUS:	*(Indifferent)* I don't know.
CAIAPHAS:	I told you not to bother them.
MALCHUS:	*(Hostile)* I didn't, but they may come anyway.
CAIAPHAS:	Well, I'm sure they will welcome the truth. Open the door!

(Malchus proceeds up the aisle and admits five members of the Sanhedrin who sit scattered throughout the audience. Malchus exits.)

CAIAPHAS:	*(Taking the judgment seat)* In your places, Scribes, Pharisees, Sadducees, Elders. Thank you for coming at this hour. We are here to examine a rabbi. He was a carpenter in Nazareth until three years ago. Now he claims to be the Son of God. Some of you have heard him. You will witness to the truth and nothing but the truth as you have heard

19

it from him. *(To members of the Sanhedrin now seated)* Two witnesses must agree. *(Joseph and Nicodemus enter at back of auditorium and move toward stage. They stand downstage right facing Caiaphas.)* Oh, Joseph and Nicodemus, I am glad you have come. We need your help to be sure everything is legal. *(Off left)* Bring in the accused! *(Annas enters from left, and Jesus is brought in by Malchus)* Who has testimony about the rabbi? *(Warningly)* Remember the law: If proven false by contrary evidence, the witness in error will be condemned. Who is the first witness?

FIRST WITNESS: *(Standing in the audience)* "I heard him say that Samaria and not Jerusalem is the place to worship." *(Sits down)*

CAIAPHAS: Is there supporting evidence? "In the witness of two shall all things be established." *(Silence)* Is there any contrary evidence? *(Silence)* Who is next?

SECOND WITNESS: *(Standing)* "I heard him say it is wrong to pay tribute to Caesar." *(Sits down)*

CAIAPHAS: Is there supporting evidence? "In the witness of two shall all things be established." *(Silence)* Is there any evidence to the contrary? *(Silence)* Next!

THIRD WITNESS: *(Standing)* "I heard him say that the Gentiles will become the Israel of God." *(Sits down)*

CAIAPHAS: Is there supporting evidence? "In the witness of two shall all things be established." No yeas? *(Pause)* Any nays? *(Pause)* Next!

FOURTH WITNESS: *(Standing)* He said, "I will destroy the temple of God, and build it again in three days." *(Sits down)*

CAIAPHAS: Is there supporting evidence?

FIFTH WITNESS: *(Standing)* I heard him say, "I will destroy the temple of God and build it again in three days." *(Sits down)*

CAIAPHAS: They agree. Does anyone question the testimony? *(Silence)* "In the witness of two shall all things be established." *(Turning left)* Rabbi, what do you say? *(Silence that baffles Caiaphas)* Do you not answer? *(Silence)* Are you silent to insult against the Temple of God, the center of our religion? *(Tense pause)* *(To the Sanhedrin)* He is silent. The charge is sustained by two witnesses. It stands legal. Is there evidence to the contrary? Joseph and Nicodemus, did you hear him say this? *(They nod assent. Silence. To Jesus)* I order you to tell us, Are you the Son of God, Rabbi?

JESUS:	I am. You will see the Son of Man sitting on the right hand of power in the clouds of heaven.
CAIAPHAS:	*(Honestly puzzled)* The Son of Man, the Son of God . . . how can this be? A carpenter, the Messiah? The human, divine? *(To the assembly)* What is your decision?
ALL:	He is false.
CAIAPHAS:	Is there one dissenting voice? *(Gestures again to Joseph and Nicodemus, who shake their heads)* There is no dissent. We shall reconvene at the break of dawn to make the sentence official, as the law requires.
MALCHUS:	*(Interrupting)* What shall I do with him—*(cynically)* Master?
CAIAPHAS:	Protect him till daybreak. *(Malchus starts to exit left with Jesus.)* Yes, protect our people from him . . . and him from our people.
MALCHUS:	I sure will. *(Pointing to his patch)* He helped me.

SCENE 2

Setting: The same
Time: At the first light of dawn, Friday morning
Scripture: Mark 15:1-15

CAIAPHAS:	*(Standing center stage at podium with gavel before the assembled ruling body—represented by the congregation or audience)* I pronounce the Sanhedrin assembled in due order. *(Pounding gavel)* Is there a quorum?
MALCHUS:	*(Counting)* There is.
CAIAPHAS:	Good. Bring the rabbi. *(Hesitating, Malchus exits left)* Honored members of the Sanhedrin, we are assembled here in due order. The number is sufficient to consider the charge against the rabbi. Some of you were at the earlier session to examine him. He claimed to be the Son of God. You will decide for yourselves if, as a carpenter and teacher, he can be. The penalty for a false claim is severe. We must protect our people against false messiahs. You understand this matter is to be cleared up before the Sabbath rest at sunset this evening. Are there any questions? *(Silence)* Bring him in! *(Malchus brings Jesus in stage left. Caiaphas sits, then speaks sadly but firmly)* Rabbi, most of these members witnessed the examination earlier this morning. They heard your

21

	claim. We shall get to the point right away. Answer once again to the question, Are you the Son of God?
JESUS:	If I tell you, you will not believe. Even though you do not, I shall be seated at the right hand of the power of God.
CAIAPHAS:	The human, divine? *(Most puzzled)*
JESUS:	Yes.
CAIAPHAS:	You say you are the Son of God then?
JESUS:	I am.
CAIAPHAS:	*(Sadly and hopelessly)* Elders of the people, you hear his claim. What is your verdict? If for life, answer, "For life." If for death, answer, "For death."
ALL:	For death. *(Caiaphas pounds gavel hard three times)*
CAIAPHAS:	We have no other course under our revered law. Take him to Pilate. The Romans insist on executing the penalty. Keep me posted, Malchus.
MALCHUS:	I will. *(Exits left with Jesus)*
CAIAPHAS:	*(Shaking his head)* The Sanhedrin is dismissed. *(Pounding gavel)* The human, divine! *(Honestly perplexed. A pause)*
ANNAS:	*(Entering downstage while shaking his head)* There seems no other way out.
CAIAPHAS:	How can the human be the divine?
ANNAS:	Even Joseph and Nicodemus agreed. There was not one dissenting voice.
CAIAPHAS:	Jesus is *not* the Messiah. *(Convinced)*
MALCHUS:	*(Entering from left. Speaking eagerly, with hope)* Your honor!
CAIAPHAS:	Yes, Malchus.
MALCHUS:	Pilate will not inflict the penalty!
CAIAPHAS:	That weasel! He promised to, if we found the rabbi false.
MALCHUS:	He told us to take the rabbi and judge him ourselves.
CAIAPHAS:	What!
MALCHUS:	We told him we have no power to carry out the sentence. That belongs to the Romans.
ANNAS:	The Gentile knows that. *(Throughout, he tries to moderate the situation)*

MALCHUS:	So he asked Jesus if he was a king.
ANNAS:	*(To Caiaphas)* From religion to politics! That pagan does not care what happens to our religion.
CAIAPHAS:	Or to our Temple . . . or people. What did the rabbi say?
MALCHUS:	That he *was* a king *(throwing up his hands),* but not of this world. Pilate said, "I find no fault in this man."
CAIAPHAS:	No fault! *(Losing control)* What about this riot in Jerusalem? Did no one mention this?
MALCHUS:	Some did. They told him that the rabbi was stirring up bloody riots from Judea to Galilee. When Pilate heard "Galilee," he sent the rabbi to Herod.
ANNAS:	*(Deeply concerned)* Pilate may let the rabbi go.
CAIAPHAS:	*(Vehemently)* He cannot do that.
ANNAS:	He will let one prisoner go. The Romans have done us this favor to celebrate our escape from Egypt.
CAIAPHAS:	*(Puzzled)* We must not let the rabbi go.
ANNAS:	Pilate does not know how serious the situation is. He knows nothing about our religion and cares less.
CAIAPHAS:	All he cares about is politics and pacifying the people.
ANNAS:	If the rabbi is let loose the people will riot. They have taken about all they can.
CAIAPHAS:	How in the world can we show Pilate their violence?
ANNAS:	I know what *may* help.
CAIAPHAS:	What?
ANNAS:	The Romans have a bad actor in jail named Barabbas. He led a riot against the Roman government and committed murder in doing it. Ask the Gentile to release Barabbas or the rabbi. Typical politician, he will not make the choice. He will let the people choose.
CAIAPHAS:	*(Doubtful)* You think they would rather free Barabbas than the rabbi?
ANNAS:	I am sure they will. This will show Pilate their hatred against the rabbi.
CAIAPHAS:	Hear that, Malchus?
MALCHUS:	*(Demurring)* Yes. Free Barabbas or the rabbi.

CAIAPHAS:	Barabbas or the rabbi. Go! *(Metronome speeds up)* We haven't much time. He must be gone before sunset. That is the law. *(Exit Malchus)* And if the people don't demand Barabbas?
ANNAS:	They will. They hate the rabbi.
CAIAPHAS:	*(Doubting)* Pilate still may not carry out the sentence.
ANNAS:	True. He has no awareness of the issues involved. Most Gentiles are blind to what a real messiah must be. *(Both exit right)*

SCENE 3

Setting: The same
Time: Later in the day
(Caiaphas stands, studying a scroll on the podium. Anna sits, ruminating. Malchus enters from left)

CAIAPHAS:	What happened?
MALCHUS:	*(Dejected)* Pilate freed Barabbas.
CAIAPHAS:	*(Jumping in)* And carried out the sentence on the rabbi?
MALCHUS:	No, he stalled again.
ANNAS:	*(Rising, speaking aggressively)* We shall have to meet him on his own ground—politics.
CAIAPHAS:	How?
ANNAS:	The rabbi says he has a kingdom.
CAIAPHAS:	A kingdom not of this world. *(Their exchange of lines is vehement and quick)*
ANNAS:	A kingdom of truth.
CAIAPHAS:	So he claims to be a king!
ANNAS:	Tell Pilate this.
CAIAPHAS:	For if the rabbi is king, Caesar is *not*.
ANNAS:	Tell him this! Tell him—Jesus or Caesar!
CAIAPHAS:	Run, Malchus. Jesus or Caesar! Time! Time!! Time!!!
	(Metronome speeds up, gets louder. Malchus exits left)
ANNAS:	This is the issue! Caesar is king or the rabbi is.
CAIAPHAS:	We know which Pilate will take.

ANNAS:	Has to take.
CAIAPHAS:	Or lose his position.
ANNAS:	And be a traitor to Rome. *(The two separate, moving to opposite sides of stage. There is a long pause to indicate passage of time)*
MALCHUS:	*(Entering dejectedly from left)* He did it!
CAIAPHAS:	Did what?
MALCHUS:	Asked the rabbi, "Are you a king?" *(Hesitant)* The rabbi said, "I am." *(Emotion mounting)* Pilate shouted, "Shall I crucify your king?" The people all yelled back, "We have no king but Caesar! Who lets the rabbi live is no friend of Caesar, no friend of Caesar!" *(Near tears, dejected)* He's on the way to Golgotha now carrying his cross. Pilate put a sign on him—"The King of the Jews"—in Greek, Latin, and Hebrew. Everyone can read it.
ANNAS:	*(Slapping his forehead)* No, not the King of the Jews!
CAIAPHAS:	He *said* he was the King of the Jews.
ANNAS:	That's the whole point.
CAIAPHAS:	If he were divine, we might have taken him. *(Conclusively)* But there was no other way out.
ANNAS:	Yes. He's too human.
CAIAPHAS:	Human enough to die before sunset? It's about nine o'clock!
MALCHUS:	Human enough to help me. *(Ripping his ear patch off. Metronome slows)*
CAIAPHAS:	*(Big sigh)* We've saved our people! From the rabbi and from rioters being killed by Romans! Go, Malchus! *(Malchus exits with Caiaphas shouting after him)* Not King of the Jews! He only said it. Thank God! *(Pounding the gavel into his hand).*
ANNAS:	Not divine enough. Too human.
CAIAPHAS:	Or is the human the divine? *(Picking up the ear patch)*
ANNAS:	Our humanness—our divineness? *(Metronome stops)*
CAIAPHAS:	Too good to be true. *(Annas and Caiaphas face each other and clasp hands, then exit downstage, start up aisle arm in arm.)*
ANNAS:	Not true. *(He and Caiaphas shake their heads)*

CAIAPHAS:	So we had to get rid of him.
ANNAS:	By his crucifixion we have saved our people. *(Halting to address each other)*
CAIAPHAS:	Saved our people by his crucifixion *(Both nod as they move forward)*
ANNAS:	His crucifixion—our salvation.
CAIAPHAS:	*(Echoing)* His crucifixion—our salvation. *(Moving up the aisle with handshake grip)*
CONGREGATION PROMPTERS:	His crucifixion, *our* salvation. *(Repeat as chant)*
TOTAL CONGREGATION:	*(Joining in)* His crucifixion, *our* salvation.
	(Rising) His crucifixion, *our* salvation.
	(Standing) His crucifixion, our *salvation.* *(Crescendo)*

Closing Hymn: "Beneath the Cross of Jesus"

The Politician—Pilate

Characters

    PILATE, the Roman governor of Judea—The Politician, wearing a bejeweled lounging jacket

    CLAUDIA, the wife of Pilate, with several sparkling bracelets on her left wrist

    MELIOR, Pilate's servant

    CAIAPHAS, the high priest

    JESUS

    JOSEPH OF ARIMATHEA

    PEOPLE, a group of choric speakers

Resources

Prop: Prisoner's chain with a few links

Music Suggestions: "Crown Him with Many Crowns," "Hallelujah Chorus" from *Messiah*, Handel; "Jesus, I My Cross Have Taken" from *The Crucifixion*, John Stainer; "Requiem," Fauré

Literature Suggestions: "Io Victis," William Wetmore Story

SCENE 1

Setting: The living room of the governor's palace in Jerusalem

Time: Late Thursday night of Holy Week

(Pilate and Claudia are lounging on a divan downstage center)

PILATE:	*(Laying his head on Claudia's lap)* I'm dead tired, Claudia.
CLAUDIA:	*(Stroking his head)* I know, darling. The atmosphere in Jerusalem is very tense.
PILATE:	Apt to blow up any second.
CLAUDIA:	*(Patting his forehead)* Today has been quiet though, Pilate. Not a murmur in the city.
PILATE:	The rabbi has been in Bethany most of the day, a couple miles out. The thunderheads always seem to gather over him. But I think I can pacify the rioters again this year.
CLAUDIA:	*(Patting his head)* I'm sure you can. You always have.
PILATE:	I may offer to release one of their own prisoners.
CLAUDIA:	Who?
PILATE:	One Barabbas. He is a Jewish rioter and a killer and is sentenced to hang tomorrow with two other criminals. He is one of their toughest. To release him may show the Jews

	our generosity. If we let one of their rebels free, we must be pretty good guys. This way they may hate us a little less.
CLAUDIA:	I wish Caesar had put Herod in charge here and set us over Galilee. This city is a red hot trouble center.
PILATE:	*(Disgusted)* Oh, Herod! He always sucks Caesar's thumb. I could never stoop to such fawning.
CLAUDIA:	Of course you couldn't. *(Thumping his chest)* You're too much of a man.
PILATE:	I'll try to handle the situation.
CLAUDIA:	I know you will. *(Starts to kiss him)*
PILATE:	Did I hear a knock? Come in. *(Caiaphas enters from right)* Oh, his honor, Caiaphas! *(Sitting up)* It is late for the high priest to be out. *(No fawning. This is no game but a confrontation of two interdependent top officials)*
CAIAPHAS:	Not too late, I hope.
CLAUDIA:	Not for *good* news, our pacifier.
CAIAPHAS:	Good evening, Claudia, honored lady. I bring good news . . . if you will make it so.
CLAUDIA:	*(Rising and moving upstage)* Better if we don't have to make it good.
PILATE:	*(Motioning to right end of divan)* Sit down. What is on your mind, Your Reverence?
CAIAPHAS:	*(Sitting on left end of divan)* Governor, if we work together we can stop a riot.
PILATE:	Barabbas's gang again?
CAIAPHAS:	No, tougher than that.
CLAUDIA:	*(Apprehensive)* The rabbi?
CAIAPHAS:	Yes. *(Firmly but matter-of-factly)* This very minute there is a riot brewing in the city. Nothing will pacify the people but his removal.
CLAUDIA:	His removal?
CAIAPHAS:	Yes. He is to be tried before the Sanhedrin within a few hours. *(Moving toward Pilate)* This is where you can help us. If he is found false, will you inflict the penalty?
CLAUDIA:	*(Interrupting with concern. She is a budding believer)* What penalty?

PILATE:	*(Disregarding her)* You say there is danger of a riot?
CAIAPHAS:	*(Exuding confidence)* Not if you work with us. The people want him out of the way. They cannot see in him a messiah. *(Touching Pilate's arm)* If he is found false and you execute the sentence, you will be idolized in the hearts of our people. You will rise in Caesar's favor, too, because you will have nipped another riot in the bud.
PILATE:	*(Vacillating)* I see no reason . . . why I should not go along. *(Patronizing)* Caesar always yields to your customs when they foster law and order.
CAIAPHAS:	*(Rising)* I knew you would help. *(Pilate rises. Caiaphas exits a step, then turns)* We may have to rouse you before dawn. Good night.
PILATE:	Good night. *(Caiaphas exits stage right)*
CLAUDIA:	*(Apprehensively)* Pilate, dear, he is using you.
PILATE:	*(Slyly)* He may be useful to me. This way I avoid responsibility. *(Smartly)* In politics you let others use you so you can use others in a pinch.
CLAUDIA:	You do that well, darling.
PILATE:	I hope Rome thinks so.
CLAUDIA:	I do. You are the best man I know.
PILATE:	Come, dear, it is late. *(They exit left)*

SCENE 2

Setting: The judgment hall of the palace
Time: Shortly after dawn on the morning of Good Friday
Scripture: Matthew 27:15-26 (Choric speakers may read at opening if
  desired)

(Throughout the scene Melior has Jesus in tow with the prisoner's chain)

PILATE:	*(Yawning repeatedly, he takes his seat center stage in the judgment hall)* Being roused out of bed to try a rabbi—Caesar will hear about this! *(Shouts off stage left)* Bring him in, Melior.
MELIOR:	*(Entering with Jesus)* The chief priests and the scribes insist that you come out to them.
PILATE:	Come out to them! What do they think I am, a puppet?
MELIOR:	They say it will make them unclean to come inside.

PILATE:	All right. *(Moving to left stage)* What charge do you bring against this man?
PEOPLE:	*(Choric speakers down left, off stage, facing Pilate)* He is guilty, or we would not have brought him to you.
PILATE:	Take him yourselves. Judge him by your laws.
PEOPLE:	We cannot execute. Rome can.
PILATE:	*(Stepping back, turning right, and speaking to Jesus)* Are you the King of the Jews?
JESUS:	Do you ask that for yourself or did others tell you?
PILATE:	Am I a Jew? I ask you about being King of the *Jews*—not *my* king.
JESUS:	You are right. Your kingdom is of this world. Mine is not. If it were, then my servants would fight so that I should not be delivered up. But my kingdom is not from hence.
PILATE:	You are a king then?
JESUS:	I am.
PILATE:	A king of what?
JESUS:	Of the truth.
PILATE:	*(Scornfully)* What is truth? Your kingdom—Caesar's kingdom, the kingdom of the Jews—my kingdom! Too many kingdoms! *(Moving toward the people)* I find no crime in him.
PEOPLE:	He stirs up *riots* from Galilee to Judea.
PILATE:	*(Shaking his head in consternation and addressing Jesus)* Do you hear what these people witness against you? *(Jesus is silent. Pilate shakes his head. Reflecting, then addressing the people)* You say he comes from Galilee?
PEOPLE:	Yes, Galilee.
PILATE:	*(Rubbing his hands dubiously)* Then take him to Herod. He is in Jerusalem right now. Galilee is his, not mine. *(Jesus is led out by Melior. Pilate sags into a chair)* What a load off my mind.
CLAUDIA:	*(Entering from right, distraught, in night robe)* Pilate!
PILATE:	What are you doing up at this hour?
CLAUDIA:	*(Clutching at him)* I just had a dream, darling.
PILATE:	What of it?
CLAUDIA:	A horrible dream, dear.

PILATE:	What about?
CLAUDIA:	That you condemned *(clutching her throat)* an innocent man . . . and suffered . . . endlessly.
PILATE:	What's in a dream?
CLAUDIA:	If the rabbi is innocent . . .
PILATE:	*(Patting her soothingly)* I will proceed slowly.
CLAUDIA:	You will?
PILATE:	Yes, dear. Go back to sleep.
CLAUDIA:	*(Holding Pilate's face in her hands, she looks lovingly into his eyes)* Do be careful, dear. *(Exits right)*

(To indicate passage of time:
Lights down. Pause. Lights up. Melior enters from left)

PILATE:	What report, Melior?
MELIOR:	Herod was glad to see Jesus. Said he had long been curious to meet the magician.
PILATE:	What did he do?
MELIOR:	He questioned Jesus, but the rabbi never said a word.
PILATE:	*(Puzzled)* His silence gets me.
MELIOR:	Herod found no fault with him.
PILATE:	As I suspected.
MELIOR:	He clothed him in purple, mocked him as a false king, and sent him back with us. He thanked you and said he valued you as his friend for life.
PILATE:	His friend? Well, that may help. *(Calculating)* With Herod on my side, I am in less danger from Rome.
MELIOR:	*(Desperate)* What shall I do with him?
PILATE:	*(Moving stage left)* Bring him on it. *(Melior brings Jesus wearing crown of thorns and purple robe at stage left)* *(Pilate speaks to the people)* You have presented this man as one that perverts the people. I examined him and found no fault in him. Herod examined him and found no fault. I cannot sentence him. He is innocent. I will whip him and let him go. Will that satisfy you?
PEOPLE:	No.
PILATE:	What will?

PEOPLE:	Keep your annual custom.
PILATE:	What custom?
PEOPLE:	Of releasing a prisoner.
PILATE:	I am. I am trying to release the rabbi to you.
PEOPLE:	Not the rabbi!
PILATE:	Who then?
PEOPLE:	Barabbas!
PILATE:	The rioter and murderer?
PEOPLE:	Yes! Barabbas!
PILATE:	*(Baffled, to Melior)* Take the rabbi out and have him whipped in their sight. That may appease them. *(Melior takes Jesus out left and sounds of lashing are heard)* I thought Barabbas was my best bet, but surely they would rather release the rabbi! *(Calling to people outside)* Whom shall I free, Barabbas *or the rabbi?*
PEOPLE:	Barabbas!
PILATE:	What shall I do *with the rabbi?*
PEOPLE:	Crucify him!
PILATE:	What evil has he done?
PEOPLE:	Let him be crucified.
PILATE:	I find no fault in him.
PEOPLE:	Away with him.
PILATE:	Behold the man!
PEOPLE:	Crucify him, crucify him!
PILATE:	Shall I crucify your king?
PEOPLE:	We have no king but Caesar.
PILATE:	Melior, water. *(Muttering)* "No king but Caesar." *(Sarcastic laugh)* I know how much Caesar is their king! *(To the people)* I wash my hands of his blood. I am innocent. *(Claudia enters right)* Claudia!
CLAUDIA:	What have you done?
PILATE:	All that I could. *(Throwing up his hands)*
CLAUDIA:	In spite of my dream?

PILATE:	Dreams? I am *governor*.
CLAUDIA:	But he's innocent.
PILATE:	So am I. *(Washes his hands apologetically)*
CLAUDIA:	I'm not. We have not heard the last of *him*.
PILATE:	I have. He's their responsibility. He's out of my way.
CLAUDIA:	*(Indicating her discipleship)* He's not out of *our* way. *(They exit right, discussing the meaning of her statement)*

SCENE 3

Setting: The living room of the governor's palace
Time: Late in the afternoon of Good Friday
Scripture: John 19:31-37

(As in Scene 1, Pilate is resting his head in Claudia's lap)

PILATE:	I have earned some peace and quiet.
CLAUDIA:	*(Caressing him)* You have had a terrible day, my dear.
PILATE:	I certainly have. I shall be glad when this Passover feast is over.
CLAUDIA:	*(A knock)* I hear someone at the door.
PILATE:	Answer it, dear. I am weary.
CLAUDIA:	*(Rising and opening the door stage right)* Melior.
PILATE:	Come in, loyal servant. No *more* trouble, I hope.
MELIOR:	The Jews want the three bodies taken down from the crosses.
PILATE:	But the bodies are not dead!
MELIOR:	No difference. The Jews are insistent. Tomorrow is Holy Day. They claim that the people will riot if the bodies are not buried before sunset.
PILATE:	Well, what can I do about it? *(Throwing up his hands)*
MELIOR:	They want the legs broken so they die faster.
CLAUDIA:	*(Cringing)* No.
PILATE:	*(Swaggering)* I hate to do that. Why add to their agony?
MELIOR:	That will shorten it. They will die sooner.
CLAUDIA:	*(Plaintively)* Can't you free him yet?

33

PILATE:	*(Disgusted)* I have begun the crucifixions and I will finish them.
CLAUDIA:	Yes, dear.
MELIOR:	*(Impatient)* What shall I tell them?
PILATE:	Tell them to go ahead. *(Moving right)* It is nothing to me. I have washed my hands of the affair. Break the legs. If you think them dead already, stab their sides. Tell the centurion. *(Melior exits)* If these Jews want their own dead, let them have their way.
CLAUDIA:	They certainly get their way with you.
PILATE:	*(Rankling under his defeat)* One would think you were the governor.
CLAUDIA:	I am only wondering about our future, darling.
PILATE:	Don't worry, Claudia. And with Herod as our friend . . . In politics you play both ends against the middle. I've let them use me. Now I've used them.
CLAUDIA:	But what about him—the man in the middle? *(Knock)*
PILATE:	The door again.
CLAUDIA:	Joseph of Arimathea.
PILATE:	Bring him in. *(Joseph enters from right carrying the chain and wristband)*
JOSEPH:	Governor! Honored lady!
PILATE:	*(Greets him politely)* It is good to see you, Joseph. You are a steadying influence among your people.
JOSEPH:	I try to do what's right.
CLAUDIA:	You have succeeded, Joseph. Everyone speaks well of you.
PILATE:	What can I do for you?
JOSEPH:	I would like to bury the body of Jesus.
PILATE:	Why do you want the body of Jesus? You are not a follower!
JOSEPH:	*(Firmly but kindly)* Yes, I am.
PILATE:	*(Amazed)* But you belong to the Sanhedrin that found him false.
JOSEPH:	Yes, but I was silent. The majority was too strong. I could not stand out for him while he was alive. But I wish to do for him what I can, now that he is dead. His Kingdom is

34

coming!

PILATE: What?

JOSEPH: The kingdom of God, Pilate.

PILATE: Oh, that! *(Someone knocks and Melior enters)* What report?

MELIOR: The legs of the men on the right and left crosses were broken. They are dying now. The one in the middle was already dead. His side was stabbed to make sure.

PILATE: *(Shaking his head in bafflement)* It usually requires a day or more for them to die. Go ahead and take the middle corpse. You can't bury the other two, can you?

JOSEPH: No, I have only one helper.

CLAUDIA: *(Pointing to wristband and chain in Joseph's hand)* Whose is that?

JOSEPH: The rabbi's.

CLAUDIA: Did he give it to you?

JOSEPH: No, I found it at the foot of the cross.

CLAUDIA: May I have it?

JOSEPH: Yes, you may.

CLAUDIA: Thank you. I will treasure it.

JOSEPH: In your palace?

CLAUDIA: On my arm *(Takes bracelets off left wrist, clamps the other on)* forever.

JOSEPH: Good evening. *(Exits right. Claudia lays her other bracelets on the table)*

PILATE: What about my bracelets?

CLAUDIA: I must wear his. *(They begin exit downstage center, moving into aisle, with her on his left arm)*

PILATE: *(Looking down at her)* But he's dead.

CLAUDIA: *(Looking up into his face as they walk side by side)* For me, never.

The Mother—Mary

Characters
MARY, the middle-aged mother of Jesus—The Mother
HANNAH, hostess in John's home at Jerusalem
JAMES, the full-grown older son of Mary
JUDA, Mary's youngest son, about eighteen
JOHN, the beloved disciple

Resources
Prop: Prayer shawls
Music Suggestions: "Ave Maria," Schubert; "Song of Mary" (Westminster Choir Series); "Maria" from *West Side Story*, Leonard Bernstein; "O Brothers, Lift Your Voices," stanzas 1 and 2; "Must Jesus Bear the Cross Alone?"

SCENE 1

Setting: John's home in Jerusalem
Time: Thursday evening, the night Jesus is betrayed
Scripture: Mark 3:19*b*-21, 31-35

There is a table center stage with benches on upstage and downstage sides. Hannah is stage right, putting a morsel of unleavened bread in a cupboard.

HANNAH:	The last bit of leavened bread for the guests. *(Knock is heard at door, stage left. Hannah bustles to the door)* Come in, Mary. We've been looking for you.

(Enter Mary with two sons, James and Juda. All three carry prayer shawls. Mary has an extra one for John)

MARY:	*(Embracing Hannah)* So good to see you.
HANNAH:	And your two sons.
JUDA:	*(Coming forward, kissing her right hand)* Good evening, Hannah!
JAMES:	*(Kissing her hand)* Good evening.
HANNAH:	How you boys have grown! James is a man now.
JAMES:	And married.
HANNAH:	You too, Juda?
JUDA:	Not yet.
HANNAH:	You are all tired from your journey. Sit down.

36

MARY:	*(Sitting on left end of upstage bench)* It is good to sit.
HANNAH:	*(Motioning to sons to sit)* Sit down too . . . men.
JAMES:	Thank you Hannah. *(In covering manner)* Is John home?
HANNAH:	Not yet.
JUDA:	Do you expect him soon?
HANNAH:	Yes. He has been spending some evenings with the Twelve in Bethany.
JAMES:	*(Registering disappointment)* Oh.
HANNAH:	He counts on your staying here. Everything is ready for you.
JAMES:	We . . . *(backs off)* Mother will explain.
HANNAH:	*(Acquiescing sweetly)* Do come back later.
JAMES:	We may.
JUDA:	Thank you, Hannah. Goodnight.
JAMES:	Goodnight. *(Both sons exit left)*
HANNAH:	Two fine boys, Mary. Where are Joses and Simon?
MARY:	They're with their families in Nazareth for Passover.
HANNAH:	*(Turns to cupboard to get bread, sets it before Mary. Sits on right end of upper bench)* Where is Jesus spending these days?
MARY:	*(Eating)* He and his disciples have been staying with Lazarus in Bethany. We stopped there but they weren't in.
HANNAH:	Oh. *(Pauses)* And James and Juda wanted to see him?
MARY:	I don't know, Hannah. *(Stopping her eating and reflecting)* I doubt it.
HANNAH:	*(With concern)* What do you mean?
MARY:	They don't know what to make of their brother.
HANNAH:	I don't understand.
MARY:	They can't see him as the Messiah.
HANNAH:	What about Joses and Simon and the girls?
MARY:	The same with them. They think of him merely as their oldest brother . . .
HANNAH:	And what do you think?
MARY:	*(Looking warily right and left before speaking)* I think he is the

Messiah, but I'm not always sure. I'm sure of this: He's the best of the good in all of us.

HANNAH: And they haven't seen this?

MARY: Yes, but they don't know if this makes him the Messiah.

HANNAH: What do they think of him?

MARY: *(Reflecting)* They think he is obsessed.

HANNAH: *(Point to her temple)* You mean "touched"?

MARY: Oh, Hannah, this is really tearing me apart.

HANNAH: What do you mean?

MARY: I love them as my children. But I love him as more than that.

HANNAH: And they don't?

MARY: *(Showing deep and long distress)* Because I love them, I want them to see in him their Messiah. *But because I believe he is more than my child,* they have turned against me. And they have turned against him as well. *(Distraught)* My family is split terribly.

HANNAH: *(Rising and comforting Mary)* Since when, Mary?

MARY: Some time ago.

HANNAH: *(Sympathetically)* And with no husband to help you.

MARY: Oh, if only he were living. He would help hold us together.

HANNAH: He's been gone a long time.

MARY: Eighteen years. All that time Jesus provided for the family. But then he became a rabbi and is gone most of the time.

HANNAH: How long has he been a teacher?

MARY: About three years.

HANNAH: Oh yes, I remember he cleansed the Temple here in Jerusalem then. That was about three years ago.

MARY: Ever since, his brothers do not want to be seen with him.

HANNAH: *(Sympathetically)* What a shame!

MARY: *(Near tears, she rises from bench and moves to front bench, sitting on left)* Things in the family have been worse since then. Once he was healing at Capernaum. His brothers suspected he was "beside himself." His enemies were getting stronger and hotter. We were afraid for his safety, so we went to bring him home. The crowd around him was so huge we couldn't get close to him. Some people told him we were there, but he didn't even come out to see us. He just went on preaching and said, "Who are my mother and my brothers? . . . Whoever does the will of God is my brother, and sister and mother."

HANNAH: That sounds strange.

MARY: It did to them, too. I believed he was honest about himself. His brothers didn't. They thought him self-possessed with his own importance.

HANNAH: So you are torn between him and them.

MARY: *(Smiling sweetly and maternally)* That was why they didn't want to stay. They don't mind being with me, but they don't want to be seen with him. When he's home we're all tense. So right now they're out trying to learn what the people think of him.

HANNAH: I don't know what to say, Mary. I'm really concerned for you.

MARY: I have no concern for myself. I love them as my sons. I believe in him as the Son of God. I pray nothing will happen to him so they will believe in him as I do.

HANNAH: *(Patting her on the shoulder)* I'm sure they will come around. They had their prayer shawls, I noticed. They will take part in the Passover here in Jerusalem, won't they?

MARY: *(With anxiety for their sakes)* What *is* the feeling about him here, Hannah?

HANNAH: *(Avoiding the question)* Let's talk about that tomorrow, Mary. You are tired now.

MARY: Yes, I am. James and Juda may come later—maybe with good news.

HANNAH: Yes, they may.

MARY: *(With anticipation)* Tomorrow I'll see him *(Pointing to shawl)* and give him this. It's been his since he was twelve.

HANNAH: I'm *sure* you will get to see him.

MARY: If only they will come to join with him.

HANNAH: Just as you do. *(With her arm around Mary's waist)* It's a blessing to have you, Mary. Let's join in the closing prayer of the Passover feast. *(Mary dons her prayer shawl and gives*

Hannah the extra one. They rise and with folded hands and with bowed heads voice their petition in unison) "Blessed art Thou, O Lord, King of the universe, who hast preserved us alive and sustained and brought us to this season."

(Hannah and Mary exit downstage center)

SCENE 2

Setting: The same
Time: The red dawn of Good Friday
Scripture: Mark 14:43-50; 15:1, 2

(Hannah stands at cupboard stage right)

MARY: *(Heard praying in hushed tones off stage)* "Hear, O Israel: the Lord our God is one Lord, and thou shalt love the Lord thy God with all thy heart, and with all thy soul, and all thy might."

(She enters stage left)

HANNAH: May it be a good feast day for you, Mary.

MARY: A glorious day to you, Hannah. Is the dawn fair?

HANNAH: It's red, I'm afraid.

MARY: *(Looking out of door stage left)* It's not too red. The day may be bright.

HANNAH: It may be. How did you rest, Mary?

MARY: Beautifully!

HANNAH: Will you have something to eat?

MARY: No. *(Returning to the table)* I think I'll keep my fast until the Passover feast this evening.

HANNAH: Come, come, that is too far off. I have baked one last morsel of leavened bread. If it is not eaten soon, we must destroy it, you know.

MARY: *(Playfully)* Very well, then, I'll join you. *(Mary sits on left end upstage bench and lays the shawl on the table. Hannah serves up muffins, sits on right end of same bench, and bows head in silent prayer, then eats)* And how did you rest, Hannah?

HANNAH: Quite well 'til midnight. After that there seemed a lot of commotion. There were people milling about in the streets until the end of the morning watch.

40

MARY:	Oh, well, that's understandable. Many visitors for the Passover had to find places to sleep in the city.
HANNAH:	But that wasn't it. It was the tramping of a *mob* with torches, swords, hoots, and shouts.
MARY:	*(With maternal concern)* I wonder what it could have been. Our people are restless and excitable during the Feast. *(With a sigh of relief)* I'm glad Jesus was out at Bethany and my other children in Capernaum.
HANNAH:	*(Looking out left window)* There comes Joseph of Arimathea, my neighbor. He's sharing his Passover lamb with us this evening. As a member of the Sanhedrin he will know what the disturbance was. *(Joseph has approached to within hailing distance)* *(Hannah calls to him off-stage left)* Joseph, is anything wrong? *(She waits for his answer and repeats his words with tense excitement)* The Sanhedrin has tried Jesus! *(Calling to him again)* Where is he? *(Again waiting for his answer as he passes)* In the hands of Herod now! *(Turning to Mary)* Did you hear that?
MARY:	*(Biting her lip)* There must be some mistake.
HANNAH:	*(With concern)* But Joseph is trustworthy. He is no newsmonger. I'll step in next door and ask him.
MARY:	*(With tenseness mounting)* Yes, do. There must be an error. Surely nothing can happen to a Messiah! *(Hannah exits left stage. Mary seats herself in controlled calmness and says to herself as if in prayer)* Another sword in my soul? His brothers and sisters—what will they think of him . . . if . . . ?Oh God, may nothing happen to him for their sakes! *(A hurried knock is heard at the door)* Come in! *(Discovering that she knows the entrant)* Oh, John.
JOHN:	Mary. *(He slowly walks up to Mary and stands absolutely still for a moment)* I have some bad news, Mary.
MARY:	*(Swallowing)* About Jesus?
JOHN:	*(Smiling as kindly as possible)* Yes. I came to tell you before you heard it some other way.
MARY:	Heard what?
JOHN:	What happened last night.
HANNAH:	*(Returning breathless from the neighbor's)* Oh, John! Is it true?
JOHN:	*(Shaking his head in sad affirmation)* I thought he would want me to tell you.

41

MARY:	*(Quietly steeling herself and sitting on right end of upstage bench)* Tell me everything. *(Hannah stands behind Mary)*
JOHN:	*(Sitting to Mary's left. With forced self-control for Mary's sake and with deliberation)* After the supper last night, Jesus led us to the Garden of Gethsemane to pray. There Judas betrayed him to the Temple guard. They bound him and led him to the high priest. In regular session at daylight this morning the Sanhedrin condemned him as a false messiah.
MARY:	*(Clutching her throat and looking off in the distance)* False!
JOHN:	*(Hurriedly with a ray of hope)* Herod or Pilate must yet pass the official sentence. They may hold out against the priests.
HANNAH:	Can nothing be done?
JOHN:	*(Calming her)* Not now. I stayed with him through it all until they turned him over to the soldiers. Then I came here. *(Bowing head in deep grief)* I love him so.
MARY:	*(Consolingly)* He loves you too, John. He's always told me that you are his beloved disciple. Where are the others?
JOHN:	Oh *(On second thought)* . . . they are safe.
MARY:	*(Rising)* I must go to him.
JOHN:	*(In firm kindness)* No, Mary. That is why I came here, to tell you that you need not be with him. I shall go back shortly, then come and tell you all that happens.
MARY:	I must see him. I'm his mother!
JOHN:	But think of him. Would he want you there? You would add to his distress.
MARY:	I'm not afraid for him either. Nothing can happen to him. He is the Messiah. I'm thinking about his brothers and sisters.
HANNAH	*(Pleading)* Do stay with me, Mary. John will tell us everything.
MARY:	I'm sure he will. But I must see for myself. He may need me now. Besides, I must tell his brothers and sisters everything.
HANNAH:	John can tell them, Mary.
MARY:	*(Sweetly and finally)* Not in a mother's place.
HANNAH:	All right, Mary. Don't forget his shawl.

JOHN:	*(Offering her his arm and leading out)* We'll be back soon.
MARY:	Thank you, Hannah. *(Talking to John as they exit and caressing his shawl)* Surely nothing can happen to their brother.

SCENE 3

Setting: At the foot of the Cross
Time: In the heat of Good Friday
Scripture: John 19:25-27

(Mary and John stand absolutely still for a minute stage left, gazing at Christ on the Cross—not a literal representation but a focus point downstage center for the actors in this scene. Then Mary, wearing the prayer shawl over her head, clutches her throat and drops her head.)

JOHN:	*(Tenderly)* We had better go now, Mary.
MARY:	*(After a long pause)* Not yet, John.
JOHN:	You believe he is the Messiah.
MARY:	*(Raising her head)* Yes, I do.
JOHN:	No one else could have said, "Father, forgive them for they do not know what they are doing."
MARY:	Umm . . .
JOHN:	Did you hear his words to the one thief?
MARY:	Yes, I did.
JOHN:	"Today you will be with me in Paradise."
MARY:	*(Slowly, with deep feeling)* How?
JOHN:	Only the Messiah could promise that.
MARY:	That's right . . . but . . .
JOHN:	*(Nodding downstage)* There is Mary Magdalene. He did so much for her.
MARY:	*(Slowly and passively)* There is your mother, Salome, too. How must she feel about you now?
JOHN:	She still has faith in me as his disciple.
MARY:	Faith in him, too?
JOHN:	*(Trying to support her with his confidence)* Yes, I'm sure.
MARY:	There's sister-in-law. How sweet of them to stand by.

JOHN:	They all loved him.
MARY:	*(With a mother's deep concern for her son)* Just so this doesn't shatter their faith in him.
JOHN:	*(Bolstering her up)* It won't. Last night in the garden he prayed for us.
MARY:	*(Reflecting)* He did!
JOHN:	We'd better go now. Hannah may get worried.
MARY:	Yes. *(Trying to edge forward)* Let me be near him for a moment . . . before we go.
JOHN:	*(Trying to shield her from the ordeal)* The crowd is packed awful close, Mary.
MARY:	We can get through.
JOHN:	Give me your hand. *(Slowly John and Mary move downstage into aisle, moving as if they worm their way through the crowd, to the foot of the cross. All the time Mary keeps looking up at her son as she haltingly follows the lead of John's hand)*
MARY:	*(Standing with John at the foot of the cross and looking up at Jesus, she whispers)* My son. *(Pause as she bows in prayer)*
JOHN:	He sees you.
MARY:	*(Looking up at him and catching her breath)* He is saying something.
JESUS:	*(Spoken by a man in the congregation or off stage)* "Woman, here is your son."
JOHN:	Did you hear that?
MARY:	Yes.
JOHN:	He wants you to stay with me.
MARY:	Pssh!
JESUS:	*(As before)* "Here is your mother."
JOHN:	He wants me to take care of you.
MARY:	*(Falling to her knees and clinging to John)* How like him to think of me, not of himself. *(Mary is sobbing. John strokes her head in sympathy)*
JOHN:	*(After understanding silence)* Whenever you are ready . . . Mother.
MARY:	*(Rising)* Yes . . . *(Reflecting)* Son. And as my son, *brother* to

44

James, Juda, and my others.

JOHN: Yes, their brother . . . through him . . . as the Messiah.

MARY: O God, may they find this, too.

JOHN: Surely they will.

MARY: *(Caressing shawl)* His. *(Draping shawl over John's shoulders)* Now yours. *(With John's arm around her waist, they trudge up the aisle)*

The Friend—Magdalene

Characters

MARY MAGDALENE, an enthusiastic young woman, cured of demons
    (perhaps manic depression)—The Friend
MARY, wife of Clopas, Joseph's brother, and mother of two or three
    disciples
SALOME, sister of the mother of Jesus, and mother of James and John
JESUS
Voices of ANNAS, JESUS, SOLDIER, and MAN IN TOMB

Resources

Prop: Gold coin purse with fringe along bottom
Music Suggestions: "The Palms" (for flute), Fauré; "Love Divine All Loves
    Excelling"; "When His Salvation Bringing"; "Ride on King Jesus"; "O
    Sacred Head Now Wounded"; "There Is a Green Hill"; "In the Garden"
    (with violin); "In Joseph's Lovely Garden," Emily Dickinson (stanzas 1
    and 2 before Scene 2, after the Scripture; stanzas 3 and 4 before Scene
    3); "Alleluia," Mozart; "I Don't Know How to Love Him," Andrew Lloyd
    Webber (verses 1 and 2 after Scene 1); "When I Survey the Wondrous
    Cross"

<u>SCENE 1</u>

Setting: Atop a hill on the road to Jerusalem
Time: The afternoon of Palm Sunday
Scripture: Mark 11:1-10

*(Trotting onto stage from the left come Mary Magdalene; Mary, the wife of Clopas;
and Salome, crowding close to the pathway, watching Jesus ride into Jerusalem in his
triumphal entry. The atmosphere is one of joy and victory. The speeches crowd in
upon each other with excitement. On right of stage all three face downstage, Mary
Magdalene between Mary on her left and Salome on her right. The movement of the
parade is from stage right to left. Magdalene carries a purse filled with coins that jin-
gle with her movements)*

MAGDALENE:	There he comes. What a crowd! *(Tingling with happiness as she clasps her fingers over her breast)* How my heart overflows with joy!
MARY C:	This is the crowning moment of my life.
SALOME:	Mine, too. *(With pardonable mother's pride, to Mary M and Mary C, who respond)* My John got the colt for him.
MAGDALENE:	*(To Salome)* The Messiah has come. *(To Mary)* His kingdom is here.

46

SALOME:	And my sons will sit on his right and his left in glory!
MARY C:	*(Proud of her boys as she crowds in front of Mary Magdalene)* Mine are loyal disciples, too. *(Pointing with right hand)* See how closely they press upon Jesus. *(Salome nods politely)*
MAGDALENE:	*(Engrossed in Jesus)* How majestically he rides! He is every inch a king! *(To her associates left, then right)* Never shall I forget the day when he came into my life.
MARY C:	*(Politely)* We all remember it.
MAGDALENE:	From deep depressions he set me free.
SALOME:	*(Plainly)* You have been loyal in helping him ever since.
MAGDALENE:	You both have given him sons. I have given him only what food and lodging we could arrange. *(In rhapsodic reminiscence)* Every hour with him and his disciples has revived that first moment.
MARY C:	*(Leading down right)* Come. Let's join the throng! *(Strains from "The Palms")*
MAGDALENE:	Yes, let's. *(Following on Mary's right, setting off slowly to right stage in the exultant throng)* What humility and what majesty. *(Salome follows Magdalene)*
MARY C:	*(Catching Magdalene's arm in excitement)* John and James are spreading their robes in his path.
SALOME:	*(Rising on tiptoes, behind Mary and Magdalene, to see and pointing out the sons of Mary of Clopas)* See your sons crowd ahead of the colt. They are laying down their robes, too.
MAGDALENE:	*(Pointing upstage right)* Look at those boys . . . Climbing the trees to break down the palm branches. What a loving tribute.
MARY C:	Listen. *(Strains from "Hosanna in the Highest" offstage)*
SALOME:	*(Trailing Mary and Magdalene and beaming with joy)* See the folks he has helped. *(Mary and Magdalene turn as Salome points them out)* The bride of Cana at whose wedding he changed the water to wine. Peter's mother-in-law, cured of fever. The paralytic carried to Jesus—see him leap and run now. The possessed man from Gadara, Lazarus!
MARY C:	*(Halting)* The procession is stopping. *(Pause)* I wonder why. *(Stretching her neck and raising on tiptoes, alarmed, to Magdalene and Salome)* It looks like some of the Pharisees.
VOICE OF ANNAS:	*(Offstage right)* Halt! Stop! Everyone! Rabbi, tell your disciples to be quiet!

VOICE OF JESUS:	*(Offstage left)* If these would hold their peace, the very stones would cry out.

(Crowd sings out "Hosanna in the Highest," fortissimo)

MAGDALENE:	If only he could touch their lives!
SALOME:	*(Enraptured)* The Messiah!
MAGDALENE:	*(Behind her associates she fingers the pouch)* How can I give this to him?
MARY C:	Oh, Magdalene, you have given him so much already. *(Magdalene fondles pouch)*
MAGDALENE:	He's worth all that I have! Come, hurry! *(Holds up her purse)* I *must* give this to him. *(All exit stage left)*

SCENE 2

Setting: Near the cross
Time: The crucifixion of Jesus
Scripture: John 19:25-30*a;* Luke 23:44-46

(Mary Magdalene, Mary Clopas, and Salome are approaching tensely from stage left. They have learned of the trial and crucifixion of Jesus and approach the scene in consternation. Magdalene carries her pouch close. The actors visualize the cross downstage center—just beyond the chancel, or just beyond edge of stage.)

MAGDALENE:	It just cannot be *true.*
SALOME:	But son John said so!
MARY C:	Where are *my* sons?
SALOME:	Where is Jesus? *(Pause)*
MAGDALENE:	*(Entering stage left and catching her breath as she sees the cross)* Is it? *(Gasping)* It is! *(Leans forward to her left and right, deciphering the title over the cross, slowly because of the distance)* "Jesus of Nazareth, King of the Jews."
SALOME:	*(Standing on tiptoes behind and between Magdalene and Mary to look through the crowd)* There is John—and sister Mary—at the foot of the cross.
MAGDALENE:	*(With deep sympathy, turning upstage, away from cross)* Why must she go through this?
SALOME:	For such a son!
MAGDALENE:	Still! *(They stand statue-like)* He is raising his head. *(Catching her throat)* His face is bloody!

48

VOICE OF JESUS:	*(In distance off right)* "Woman, here is your son. Here is your mother."
SALOME:	Thinking of his mother. *(Weeping)* Sister!
MARY C:	She would have us think of him.
MAGDALENE:	*(Embracing both)* And not of herself.
SALOME:	*(Between sobs)* My son—a home for her. *(In distress, looking at cross)* Is this his place in the Kingdom? No!
MARY C:	John will take care of her.
SALOME:	*(As if talking to herself)* In Jesus' place . . .
MAGDALENE:	*(Fingering the pouch and thinking aloud)* How can I use this for him now? *(Pause)* Let's move to the edge of the crowd. It would add to his suffering to see us. *(They work their way stage left)* The sun is high. *(She wipes her brow then sits down center stage, nearest of the three to the cross. Mary and Salome sit too. Pause.)*
MARY C:	*(Looking up behind her)* A cloud is coming up. *(Thunder— produced by shaking a sheet of metal)*
SALOME:	*(Alarmed)* It's more than a cloud. *(Thunder)*
MAGDALENE:	It's growing dark! *(Lights dim. Loud and long thunder. The voice of Jesus is heard off right, "My God, why have you forsaken me?")* Has God forsaken him? I can't believe it. No! *(Pause, then lights come up)*
MARY C:	*(Looking stunned)* The sun is halfway down. It must have been dark for almost three hours. The crowd is gone.

(Mary Magdalene rises with eyes fixed on the cross, draws nearer to it. So do Mary C and Salome.)

SALOME:	Listen!
VOICE OF JESUS:	"I thirst." *(Mary Magdalene starts toward cross)*
MARY C:	Wait. *(Gently catching left arm)* One of the soldiers is giving him vinegar.
MAGDALENE:	*(Pausing to watch soldier)* But he is so crude; his reed, so hard.
SALOME:	Must he die? He helped so many!
MAGDALENE:	*(In distress of doubt)* The kingliest of men. The humblest, the mightiest, the best.
VOICE OF JESUS:	"It is finished!"

49

SALOME:	*(Heaving a sigh of relief)* Thank God! *(The three enfold each other in tears)*
VOICE OF JESUS:	"Father, into your hands I commend my spirit." *(Rumbling offstage)*
MARY C:	"Father"—not forsaken! *(Dramatic pause) (To Magdalene)* What will happen to the bodies?
MAGDALENE:	They must not be left hanging over the Sabbath. *(Stepping right)* His body! *(Fingering her pouch)* How can I use this for him?
MARY C:	Here come two men.
MAGDALENE:	Dressed like members of the Sanhedrin . . .
MARY C:	That condemned him false.
MAGDALENE:	*(Astonished, gazing off right)* Surely no one of them would bury him!
MARY C:	*(Looking right)* They don't seem bent on desecration. They're talking to the soldiers.
MAGDALENE:	*(Pause)* Now they're taking the body down. *(Starting down-stage)* Maybe I can help.
MARY C:	Stay, Magdalene.
MAGDALENE:	If only I could do something.
MARY C:	*(First peering right to left)* Do they have far to go?
MAGDALENE:	*(Pointing upstage right)* There is a garden up the path. Will they stop there? Yes.
MARY C:	*(Rising to leave)* There. The stone is in place. The sun is setting over the rim of the hills. Let us go . . . before darkness comes.
MAGDALENE:	Or *has* darkness come? *(Rises. Opens the pouch and takes out a few coins. Struck with a new idea)* I'll buy some spices to anoint his body at dawn on the first day of the week!
MARY C:	*(Weakened with grief)* At his tomb!
MAGDALENE:	As soon as daylight comes. *(Catches the meaning of her own words)* Daylight . . . come? *(Holds up purse)* With him . . . dead? *(All exit stage left)*

SCENE 3

Setting: Near the tomb of Jesus
Time: The dawn of the first Easter
Scripture: Mark 16:1-8

(It is hardly light enough to see. Moving up the aisle to the front of stage, Mary Magdalene, her feet stockinged, tiptoes toward the tomb with fear and anxiety. As she fondles the pouch, both hands at her bosom, she takes a few steps, then peers upstage through the dimness, but still cannot locate the tomb, which is located upstage center. She takes a few more steps, then gasps.)

MAGDALENE: The stone . . . is moved! *(She advances another step or two, then cries)* NO! *(She drops the pouch as she stoops to look into the tomb. She sees nothing and rises. Her words increase in volume as she shouts to herself)* The . . . body . . . is gone! *(Hurries off downstage left)*

(Tense voices are heard in aisle approaching stage)

MARY C: Do you have spices? *(Pause)*

SALOME: Yes, you too?

MARY C: Yes, I bought them after his burial.

SALOME: I'm sure Magdalene will bring some.

MARY C: She always does more than her share.

SALOME: *(Walking toward the stage)* Come on. It's light enough now.

MARY C: *(In practical tone)* Who will move the stone?

SALOME: I hadn't thought of that.

MARY C: *(Disappointed)* We can't budge it!

SALOME: Even with Magdalene.

MARY C: *(Kneeling to look toward the tomb)* But look!

SALOME: What?

MARY C: The stone!

SALOME: What of it?

MARY C: It's been moved!

SALOME: *(Taken aback)* It has!

MARY C: *(Wide-eyed)* We saw the men put it in place.

SALOME: Is the body there?

MARY C:	Let's see. *(She tiptoes forward cautiously and peers into tomb)*
MAGDALENE:	*(Calling from distance offstage left)* Salome! *(Enters)*
SALOME:	*(Turning)* Magdalene, where have you been?
MAGDALENE:	I was here earlier.
MARY C:	*(Coming onto stage)* The tomb is open, Magdalene!
MAGDALENE:	*(Mysteriously)* Yes, I know.
SALOME:	Did you roll the stone back?
MAGDALENE:	No.
SALOME:	Who could have done it?
MARY C:	We saw the men shove it in place after the burial.
MAGDALENE:	And I was told last night that the Sanhedrin posted guards here. Have you looked in?
MARY C:	I was just going to.
MAGDALENE:	Should we?
MARY C:	*(Leading way as Magdalene and Salome follow)* Let's try. *(The three very slowly edge up stage and stoop to look in)* A young man!
MAGDALENE:	Jesus?
MARY C:	No.
SALOME:	*(Running away)* Oh, Magdalene! *(Retreating a few steps)* Oh, my goodness!
MARY C:	Hush!
VOICE:	Do not be amazed. *(All three retreat from the tomb as the voice comes from backstage)* You seek Jesus of Nazareth who was crucified? He has risen. He is not here. See the place where they laid him. *(The three women edge upstage very gingerly, stand stone still, express amazement on their faces with hands extended, then retreat as stealthily as they had advanced. The voice speaks firmly)* Go, tell his disciples and Peter that he is going before you to Galilee; there you will see him, as he told you.
MAGDALENE:	Galilee! That's where he first found me.
MARY C:	Tell his disciples.
SALOME:	And Peter!
MARY C:	*(Returning to pick up pouch)* Is this yours, Magdalene?

MAGDALENE:	Yes. *(Taking it tenderly)* Thank you. How can I give it to him now?
SALOME:	Do you think he may be alive?
MAGDALENE:	Could a person like him stay dead?
MARY C:	He was dead.
SALOME:	Yes, he was.
MAGDALENE:	He may not be . . . now! *(To Mary C, Salome, and to herself, very deliberately)* He . . . may . . . be *(She can't say it)* He may be . . . ALIVE!
MARY C AND SALOME:	*(Separately)* Alive? Alive!
MAGDALENE:	If he is, this *(holding out purse)* is his! *(Clutching her purse to her heart, indicating her heart and so herself)* And I . . . am his.
MARY C AND SALOME:	*(Separately)* So am I.
MAGDALENE:	If . . . if . . . *(Three exit up aisle, Magdalene trailing. There is a long pause)*

(Violin or other instrument plays "In the Garden" in the background. Magdalene enters, coming down the aisle, weeping. Edging slowly and tiptoeing onstage she stoops to look into the tomb. She succumbs to grief and slumps to her knees. Jesus enters right in white shroud, moving slowly toward Magdalene. In silence he watches her weeping)

JESUS:	*(Sympathetically)* Woman, why do you weep?
MAGDALENE:	*(Barely lifting her head, then looking down again)* Have you carried him away? *(Looking around)* Where have you laid him? *(She looks at him in the quest but again lowers her head in grief)*
JESUS:	*(Pause)* M-A-R-Y.
MAGDALENE:	*(Turning to face Jesus and still kneeling looks up at him)* MASTER! *(She extends her arms and raises herself up to embrace him in profile)*
JESUS:	*(Barely raising his hands to halt her)* Not now, Mary. *(She withdraws her arms and sags back to kneeling position)* I must ascend. *(Extends his hands in blessing her)* Go and tell my disciples I will ascend to my Father.
MAGDALENE:	Ascend?
JESUS:	Yes, to my Father and to *your* Father.
MAGDALENE:	*(Leaving her purse at Jesus' feet, she rises slowly as if from a trance, turns facing downstage. Momentarily she stands*

entranced) I *saw* him. He . . . is . . . alive! *(She exits up center aisle slowly at first, then more quickly)* He lives! *(Excited)* He LIVES!

(Jesus picks up her purse, strokes it, then gently lays it on the communion table, if there is one, or back on the ground. He exits in stately silence up center aisle)

Mozart's "Alleluia" or Handel's "Hallelujah Chorus"

The Skeptic—Thomas

Characters
THOMAS, the last of the eleven to believe—The Skeptic
MATTHEW, Thomas's associate among the twelve
LAZARUS, the friend Jesus raised from the dead
JESUS, after the Resurrection

Resources
Prop: Black pinhole disk for Thomas
Music Suggestions: "The Strife Is O'er"; "Christ the Lord Is Risen Today";
   "Hallelujah Chorus" from the *Messiah,* Handel; "He Lives, He Lives"
Literature Suggestions: "Rabbi Ben Ezra," Robert Browning (stanza 3)
   "In Memoriam," Alfred Tennyson (stanzas 1–4)

SCENE 1

Setting: Living room of Mary and Martha in Bethany, two chairs center
Time: Late Thursday night after the arrest of Jesus
Scripture: John 11:5-7, 14-16

(Thomas and Matthew have just entered, disheveled, distracted, and dejected. Thomas is thinking through their dilemma in silence. Throughout, he wears a black pinhole disk on a cord used centuries ago and today to focus vision. Occasionally he puts it to his eye and scrutinizes through it. They enter left into the living room in the home of Mary and Martha.)

MATTHEW: *(Sighs)* Oh! In a safe place once more, Thomas, among friends.

THOMAS: *(Sitting down and speaking with apprehension. His lines are short and deliberate)* Unless the Temple guards pursue us tomorrow.

MATTHEW: I was sure scared they might grab us before we escaped from the garden.

THOMAS: Our turn may still come.

MATTHEW: *(Sitting and shaking his head in despair)* This means the end of him, I'm afraid.

THOMAS: I'm afraid so, too. *(In deep thought)*

MATTHEW: And of our discipleship?

THOMAS: I suspect.

MATTHEW: And of the Kingdom.

THOMAS: No doubt.

55

MATTHEW:	What will they do with him? *(Waiting in vain for a response from Thomas)* They had clubs and blades and bound him with shackles.
THOMAS:	He's in their clutches now.
MATTHEW:	I suppose we should have gone with him. But he didn't seem to want us in danger. He went ahead to meet the guards and left us behind. He made it easy for us to escape.
THOMAS:	Yes, he did.
MATTHEW:	I admire Peter, though, for the way he drew out his blade and struck the servant of the high priest. Do you suppose all of us could have defended the rabbi if we had drawn ours? *(Waits for an answer, but receives none)* They outnumbered us at least five to one. What will they do with him?
THOMAS:	What happens to a lamb among wolves?
MATTHEW:	*(Biting his lips and hesitating to say)* Do you think so? *(No answer)* To the Messiah?
THOMAS:	I fear the worst for him.
MATTHEW:	*(Reminiscing)* That day he said, "Follow me" I closed up my tax booth and followed him. I remember it as if it were yesterday. It's been about three years. Must I return to tax collecting again? What are you going to do, Thomas?
THOMAS:	Nothing—for the present.
MATTHEW:	Where are the other disciples? I last saw Peter and John trailing the mob down to the city. But James, Andrew, Philip and the others—where are they? We should have bumped into them in the garden.
THOMAS:	I didn't see them at all.
MATTHEW:	*(Confidentially)* Who would have thought it of Judas? With a kiss!! I never suspected him, did you?
THOMAS:	No, I didn't.
MATTHEW:	Should I waken Lazarus and tell him what happened? *(Pause, but no answer)* He and his sisters will want to know.
THOMAS:	Maybe so.
MATTHEW:	Do you think I should?
THOMAS:	*(Mumbling)* Uhmm. *(Rising and offering to go)* I'll tell him.
MATTHEW:	*(Rising and going)* I'll do it.

THOMAS: *(Watching Matthew go off right stage, then sitting down again. A long weighty silence. Then in complete disgust and painful self-analysis)* What a wretch I am. We tried to stop him from coming to Jerusalem. When he insisted on coming, I stated boldly, "Let us also go, that we may die with him." I meant it—then *(Pause)*. But when danger to him threatened my life, I fled like a scared quail. What a coward—yes, traitor worse than Judas I turned out to be. *(Pause)* He is in the clutches of the enemy. I am under the roof of friends. *(Ironically against himself)* "Let us also go, that we may die with him." Thomas, did you mean it? *(Rising and trudging to and fro)* If you did, you can't stay here. You must go out where he is—risk your life with him, if you belong to him. *(Pause in the agony of mental struggle)* When I volunteered to die with him, I thought I *did* mean what I said. I *did* love him. But was it all a mirage in the desert? *(Sitting with chin in hand)* I can't square his death with being the Messiah. *(Nodding his head in consternation)* At the supper *this* evening he said, "I go to prepare a place for you . . . I am the way, the truth, and the life." *(In agony of soul)* They may kill him. *(Rising and stalking left—then stalking right)* Is death the truth? *(Stamping foot)* Is death—life? I can't see it. *(Sitting, drops his head in prayer)* Father, God, he taught us to pray, your will be done. Is his death your will, his way . . . the way for me? How is he the way, the truth, and the life? *(Raising his head and acknowledging his friend who has returned)* Yes, Matthew.

MATTHEW: *(Returning from right stage)* Lazarus is going to the city right away.

THOMAS: *(Pauses a moment before answering decisively)* He is? That's rushing into needless danger. He'd better be careful! I'll stay here *(putting disk to his eyes)* until I see my way clear. *(With sincere finality)* If he is the Messiah, he can't be done away with. If he is done away with, then I'm lost. *(Walking heavily off stage left. Matthew slowly follows, shaking his head)*

SCENE 2

Setting: The same
Time: Late in the evening of the first Easter
Scripture: John 20:19-25

(Entering from left Thomas and Lazarus are discussing the news of the resurrection. Thomas's hair is still disheveled, and his face tense with weariness)

57

THOMAS:	I wish I could believe it, Lazarus *(Pause)*, but I can't.
LAZARUS:	I too wish you could. If you had been raised from the dead as I was, you would believe it. There is but the width of a hair between life and death.
THOMAS:	I can understand how he raised you. *(Lifting disk to right eye)* I saw that with my own eyes. But with him gone, the life-giver is gone.
LAZARUS:	*(Looking toward door)* Matthew left this morning to check on the empty tomb. He should be back soon.
THOMAS:	If the guards do not grab him.
LAZARUS:	They may.
MATTHEW:	*(Bursting into the room from left)* He's alive!
THOMAS:	*(Baffled)* What?
MATTHEW:	He showed himself to us.
THOMAS:	*(Recovering self-possession)* Where?
MATTHEW:	In the Upper Room.
THOMAS:	*(Stricken)* Where we had the supper?
MATTHEW:	Yes! We were sitting around that table and all of a sudden Jesus was there with us.
THOMAS:	Tell me exactly what happened.
LAZARUS:	Yes, tell us.
MATTHEW:	I'm so excited, I don't want to get it jumbled. *(Sitting)* We heard this morning, you know, that Mary Magdalene and the other women had found the tomb empty.
THOMAS:	Yes, and they said they had seen a *man* in it.
MATTHEW:	. . . who said that Jesus was risen.
THOMAS:	But they did not see him.
MATTHEW:	Right. So we hiked out to the city right away.
THOMAS:	*(Dejectedly)* I should have gone with you.
MATTHEW:	We went to the Upper Room in Mark's home. There we felt safe. Peter and John were there. They had been at the tomb early that morning and found it as Magdalene had said—empty.
THOMAS:	But no *man* inside?

MATTHEW:	Right. No man inside.
THOMAS:	Conflicting reports here.
MATTHEW:	But John believed that Jesus was risen. Peter did not know what to make of it. Shortly afterward, Magdalene came in. She said . . . she had seen . . . Jesus . . . *alive.*
THOMAS:	*(Intensely)* Just what did she say? How did she know it was he?
MATTHEW:	She didn't. At first sight she thought it was the gardener.
THOMAS:	First she thought he was the gardener, then she thought he wasn't.
MATTHEW:	*(Interrupting)* Then Jesus called her name—"Mary"—and she recognized him.
THOMAS:	*(Thinking aloud)* First she did not know him; then she did.
MATTHEW:	Right away Peter left and went to the tomb once again.
LAZARUS:	Alone?
MATTHEW:	Yes. But he had been gone only a short while when he dashed breathless into the room again.
LAZARUS:	Yes?
MATTHEW:	And what do you think had happened? Peter, too, had seen Jesus alive.
THOMAS:	*(Feeling his way slowly, but securely)* So the tomb *is* empty.
MATTHEW:	*(Enthusiastically)* Yes, we are sure of that. Magdalene and others insisted it was. We also went out toward evening and found the body gone.
THOMAS:	*(Keenly analyzing)* But you say that only Magdalene and Peter saw him alive.
MATTHEW:	No. While we were talking in the Upper Room, Clopas with a friend rushed in from Emmaus. He had Jesus as his supper guest that afternoon.
THOMAS:	Did they notice his hands?
MATTHEW:	I suppose so, I didn't ask.
LAZARUS:	Now what about his appearance to you in the Upper Room?
MATTHEW:	We were sitting there talking together about how wonderful it would be if he were alive. Peter and John were sure that he was. The men from Emmaus were sure. The rest of us wanted to be, but it seemed too good to be true. Then

all of a sudden like the dawning of day Jesus was there. Very quietly, he said "Peace be with you." We froze speechless as statues. We thought he was a ghost. As if reading our thoughts, he said, "Behold my hands and my feet. It is I myself. Handle me and see that I have flesh and bones."

THOMAS: *(Avidly)* Did you touch him?

MATTHEW: *(With strong confidence)* No. We were that sure it was he!

THOMAS: You didn't touch him? How long did he stay?

MATTHEW: Not very long. Once again he said, "Peace be with you." *(Opening his hand into the air)* After that he was gone.

THOMAS: *(Sick with regret)* I wish I had been there.

MATTHEW: I wish so too, for your sake. Then you would be as sure as we are. *(Hurriedly)* I must go and tell Mary and Martha. *(Exits left)*

LAZARUS: *(Lovingly and with patience)* You cannot doubt it now, Thomas.

THOMAS: I'm still not sure!

LAZARUS: But you can take Matthew's word. He was there.

THOMAS: I don't doubt Matthew, Peter, John, or the other disciples. I believe they saw him. But that does not make me sure.

LAZARUS: But the Master told us to live by faith.

THOMAS: Yes, by faith in *him*, not by faith in *them*.

LAZARUS: But it seems to fit, that the Lord of Life should win over death.

THOMAS: But fitness is not certainty, Lazarus. Too much hinges on it. If he has risen, then the kingdom of God is spiritual, not political as our leaders expect it to be. Then they are wrong and we have to tell them they are wrong. Then they will persecute us—yes, they may crucify *us*. That is nothing. *(Pause)* I still say, "Let us also go, that we may die with him." But I want to know beyond the shadow of a doubt before I court death.

LAZARUS: The disciples saw him alive.

THOMAS: I know they did. But how do I know that his resurrection was not merely spiritual? Do you remember what Matthew said? *(Significantly)* No one touched his body. I can't believe until *(putting disk to his eye)* I see the scars of the nails in his hands, put my fingers into those scars, and

	thrust my hand into his side.
LAZARUS:	But how could his resurrection be only spiritual? Without death there can be no resurrection. But his soul never died; so his resurrection could not be spiritual. He died physically. His body was buried. He must have risen physically because the tomb is empty.
THOMAS:	But so is yours, Lazarus. You will die again. Will he?
LAZARUS:	You're too deep for me, Thomas.
THOMAS:	*(In travail)* I wish that I could believe it. But one cannot honestly accept a thing just because one wishes to.
LAZARUS:	But as long as a man is honest in his thinking, he will find the truth.
THOMAS:	*(Holding out his disk)* I must see the truth before I can believe it.
LAZARUS:	I heard the disciples talk about gathering in the Upper Room on the first day of the next week. Meet with them, Thomas. He may appear again.
THOMAS:	*(Arguing with himself)* But if he is body, where is he? If he is spirit, why does he not show himself now? Is he limited to the first day of the week? To the Upper Room?
LAZARUS:	*(Humbly)* I do not know.
THOMAS:	If I could only see him. This uncertainty is tearing me apart. *(Both exit left)*

SCENE 3

Setting: The Upper Room in Jerusalem with a table and benches
Time: The evening of the Sunday after Easter
Scripture: John 20:26-29

(Matthew and Thomas enter from left. Imagine the other disciples seated at center table)

MATTHEW:	Fellow disciples, Thomas has come with me. He has been haunted by uncertainty all week. We know the distress he feels.
THOMAS:	If you have stayed on in Jerusalem for my sake, I'm sorry to have detained you. I appreciate your concern.
MATTHEW:	We only hope we can be of help to you, Thomas. We had our misgivings before we saw him.

61

THOMAS:	*(Advancing to center stage as he addresses the group)* I trust I do not seem stubborn. The bodily resurrection of Jesus is for me a matter of life or death. Once I am convinced of it nothing can cause me to waver. But to be sure, I must see him!
JESUS:	*(Enters from right and extends hand in blessing)* Peace be with you, Thomas. *(The hush of silence as Thomas moves very slowly downstage to right. He is taken aback and slowly drops to his knees as Jesus calls his name)* Thomas, put your finger here and see my hands. Put out your hand in my side. Do not be faithless, but believing.
THOMAS:	*(Partially rising, he lifts up his hands to touch Jesus, but before doing so sinks back into kneeling position)* My Lord and my God.
JESUS:	*(In warm appraisal)* That is the noblest confession ever made of me, Thomas.
THOMAS:	*(Whispering)* Alive in spirit *and in body!*
JESUS:	Because you see, you believe. Blessed are those who do not see and yet believe.
THOMAS:	*(Rising in throes of discovery)* Is faith without sight . . . better . . . than faith with sight?
JESUS:	Yes, Thomas. *(Jesus quietly exits right)*
THOMAS:	*(Gasping and rising)* He is gone. *(Turning to Matthew)* But how can . . . faith . . . be better . . . than sight?
MATTHEW:	Because faith gives *insight* that sight alone does not give.
THOMAS:	I needed insight, you say? Say that again.
MATTHEW:	*(Very slowly)* Faith gives insight that sight alone does not give.
THOMAS:	Insight is what I needed, you say?
MATTHEW:	Yes. This is what counts.
THOMAS:	But can't sight *(holding up disk)* give insight better than faith can?
MATTHEW:	Not always, Thomas. Even sight requires faith. It takes faith—to put together what you see—to give it meaning. This is insight.
THOMAS:	*(Relieved, exultant) I see!* Insight *is* what counts. Sight without faith does not give it, but faith without sight does.

MATTHEW:	And insight is open to everyone, not only to us who could touch him.
THOMAS:	*(Amazed at himself)* I didn't touch him myself, did I?
MATTHEW:	Yet you believe he arose.
THOMAS:	Yes, I do.
MATTHEW:	And you are sure he is alive.
THOMAS:	Yes . . . alive forever, not to die again.
MATTHEW:	Even though you can't see him now.
THOMAS:	Yes, I believe he is.
MATTHEW:	You see, Thomas, faith is greater than his empty tomb you can see or his body you can touch. It is your bond with him, person to person.
THOMAS:	I see *(smiling)* . . . even though I don't see how now. Seeing isn't always believing, but believing is always seeing.
MATTHEW:	You've got it, Thomas.
THOMAS:	Now I see him—*through* death—as the way, the truth, and the life.
MATTHEW:	Great!
THOMAS:	I once said, "Let us also go, that we may *die* with him!"
MATTHEW:	Are you less afraid to die now?
THOMAS:	You know *what* I feel now?
MATTHEW:	No, Thomas.
THOMAS:	Let us go that we may *live (Rips his pinhole disk from around his neck and throws it backstage)* with him. Let's go . . . *with* him. *(Thomas extends right arm to Matthew and they dash off downstage, up center aisle)*